Sum

of

The ONE Thing
Gary Keller & Jay Papasan

Conversation Starters

By BookHabits

Tips for Using BookHabits Conversation Starters:

EVERY GOOD BOOK CONTAINS A WORLD FAR DEEPER THAN the surface of its pages. The characters and their world come alive through the words on the pages, yet the characters and its world still live on. Questions herein are designed to bring us beneath the surface of the page and invite us into the world that lives on. These questions can be used to:

- Foster a deeper understanding of the book
- Promote an atmosphere of discussion for groups
- Assist in the study of the book, either individually or corporately
- Explore unseen realms of the book as never seen before

About Us:

THROUGH YEARS OF EXPERIENCE AND FIELD EXPERTISE, from newspaper featured book clubs to local library chapters, *BookHabits* can bring your book discussion to life. Host your book party as we discuss some of today's most widely read books.

Table of Contents

Introducing *The ONE Thing*

*T*he ONE Thing by Gary Keller and coauthored with Jay Papasan has become one of the highest bestselling books in 2018. Through tested theories to help one become less distracted and more focused, readers will be able to find how to reach their goals. No matter how one measures their success, whether professional or personal, the ability to lose distractions and focus on their ONE Thing is what will help them reach extraordinary results.

Everyone needs help to reach their goals every now and then. *The ONE Thing* by Gary Keller and Jay Papasan will be the guide that many will be turning to when a person is having a difficult time reaching their goals. Keller and Papasan go over the benefits of making a single task their priority and how to engage in that singular task with a strong focus. The first section, entitled "The Lies: They Mislead and Derail Us," helps one realize that multitasking may not be the best way to go about work, despite it being a desirable trait in many jobs. Keller and Papasan also go over the idea of having a balance between life and work, while being ideal, isn't realistic. It is all to often that home-life will bleed into work-life, despite one's best efforts to keep it from doing so. The second section follows the previous by working with the principals of productivity such as making benchmarks and building good habits. Keller and Papasan go over how readers can figure out the one thing they can do that will help make everything else either easier, or completely unnecessary. The author duo suggest that readers should work on engaging their One Thing at least four hours every day to help make it habitual and part of their everyday life. Following the economist Vilfredo Pareto's philosophy of twenty percent effort producing eighty percent of the results, readers will learn that through engaging in their one important task will be able to produce their desired results without them having to put in too much effort. Keller and Papasan realize that everyone's life is different and will need different goals. Their book goes over what the difference between the big-picture One Thing and the small-picture One Thing; what is a person's One Thing is for their life, and what a person's One Thing is at the moment. Their main idea for this is that trying to focus on multiple tasks will end up creating to discord in a person's life as well as poor performance. The last section of *The ONE Thing* discusses "Extraordinary Results," and how to use the previously discussed principals and theories in action. One of the main topics within this section is the concept of blocking out sections of time that is to be used for a person's One Thing. Each section of time should contain your One Thing, a time to relax, a time to plan and a time to reflect. If something happens during your previously scheduled time block, it is considered a distraction and must be rid of. Keller and Papasan realize that not everyone has time to re-read their book if they have forgotten how to follow their suggestions. With that in mind, each section will have a summery at the end to help refresh one's memories and reflect on what had been previously taught.

Of course, a self-help and motivational book such as *The ONE Thing* would be useless if the authors themselves couldn't endorse their work. Gary Keller himself is known to follow his own teachings that are within his and Jay Papasan's book and wants to help others find success just as they have. While many have thought of success as being perfect, Keller knows that isn't the case. He understands that a completely distraction-free day is impossible and unrealistic. Instead he hopes that through this book, readers will be able to learn what it is that matters most and through learning their One Thing, they will be able to eliminate distraction while they are focusing on it. One suggestion Keller makes is to think of a person's One Thing being like going to see a movie; one will turn off their phones, grab all of their snacks and will use the restroom before the movie starts just so the person can have a uninterrupted experience. By using this same focus for a person's One Thing, amazing things can happen and that person will have a more fulfilled and happy life. You are the person that knows yourself the best. What is your one goal, your One

Thing, that you could do to make the rest the areas of your life easier? It may not necessarily be just one step in your life, but a series of One Things that sequentially create your best self.

Discussion Questions

"Get Ready to Enter a New World"

Tip: Begin with questions dealing with broader issues to ensure ample time for quality discussions. Read through all discussion questions before engaging.

~~~

question 1

Gary Keller and Jay Papasan suggest that one should focus on One Thing. What could this mean for you in your life?

~~~

question 2

By focusing on your One Thing, Keller and Papasan
state that your life will be subsequently easier.
How do you think that is?

~ ~ ~

~~~

question 3

Keller uses the analogy of going to see the movie as a way to show how people should focus on their One Thing. Do you think this is a good analogy? Why or why not?

~~~

question 4

Keller stated that your One Thing may be a series of steps, rather than only one step. What steps would be your One Thing to make your goal?

~~~

question 5

Keller and Papasan state that distractions are something to be rid of when working on your One Thing. What are some of the distractions that are taking away from your One Thing's time block?

~ ~ ~

question 6

Keller and Papasan state that a person should block their time to better work on their goal. What would you block your time with? What would you be focusing on within those time blocks?

question 7

One of the theories that Keller and Papasan has is that multitasking isn't a good habit. Why do you think that is?

~~~

question 8

Keller and Papasan use the economist Vilfredo Pareto's philosophy of 20% makes 80% of the results. Do you think this is valid? Why or why not?

question 9

Keller and Papasan suggest that a person should block at least four hours to work on their One Thing. Do you think this is reasonable? Why or why not?

~~~

question 10

Keller and Papasan state that the idea of a balanced work-home life isn't realistic. Why do you think that is? Is it possible to achieve the perfect balance? Why or why not?

~~~

~~~

question 11

Keller and Papasan state that there are multiple ways to measure success. What are some ways that you measure success?

~~~

~~~

question 12

Something that this book goes over is the lies that get in the way of our One Thing. What do you think that means? What lies are getting in the way of your One Thing?

~~~

~~~

question 13

This book goes over time thieves that keep
someone from reaching and doing their One Thing.
What is a time thief for you? How will you get rid
of the thief in your life?

~~~

question 14

One of the blocks of time that Keller and Papasan suggest is to have a block for reflection. What would you interpret this block as? What would you reflect upon?

~ ~ ~

question 15

Keller states that he follows his own theories that he has written about within this book. Do you think that makes this book for valuable? Why or why not?

~~~

question 16

One reviewer stated that this book is a "standard operating procedure" for someone who is looking to add more productivity and purpose to their life. Do you think this is valid? Why or why not?

~~~

~~~

question 17

One reviewer stated that this book is more about the journey, than the end goal. Do you think this reviewer is correct? Why or why not?

~~~

~~~

question 18

One reviewer stated that the strategies within *The ONE Thing* are "painfully obvious". Do you agree? Why or why not?

~~~

question 19

One reviewer stated that what they got from *The ONE Thing* is to see look where you have the most success, distill your actions to the most powerful one and then to remove everything else. Do you think this is valid? Why or why not?

~~~

question 20

One reviewer stated that despite the books appealing energy and style, more intellectual substance would have been desired within the book. Do you think this would have helped the book as well? Why or why not?

~~~

Introducing the Author

As the authors of *The ONE Thing*, Gary Keller and Jay Papasan are no strangers to being a successful entrepreneur. Both writers have worked hard and succeeded within their respective circles before they came together to write *The ONE Thing*.

Gary Keller is most known for being the founder and chairman for the Keller Williams Realty. Being one of the world's largest real estate franchises, Keller had to make sure his company runs efficiently. Before he created Keller Williams Realty, Keller started at a company that would later become his competition. Within this company.

Keller had the desire to work his way to the top as a Vice President. However once he made that goal, he realized he no longer wanted to work at that company. Instead he wanted to create his own real estate company where the agents came first and to create a more positive view with the community. Thus, in 1983, Keller Williams Realtors was born with his partner Joe Williams. With his hard work, Keller became a finalist for *Inc. Magazine*'s Entrepreneur of the Year award due to leading his company successfully for thirty years and being one of the most influential leaders within the real estate world. Keller Williams Realtors has also recently announced that they would be expanding internationally to France, Poland, Nicaragua, Israeli and Monaco. Something that makes Keller Williams Realtors different from other companies is its focus on education and the tools that are provided within the company. While Keller and his associates worked on updating their educational tools for their agents, they chose to put their teachings on paper so others could be just as successful. Gary Keller then wrote about his success as a real estate agent which became his three other bestsellers: *The Millionaire Real Estate Investor, The Millionaire Real Estate Agent* and *SHIFT: How Top Real Estate Agents Tackle Tough Times.* Despite his monumental success within the business world, Keller is known to see his biggest achievement in his life to being the world he has created with his wife and son.

Jay Papasan has been working with books most of his career after graduating from New York University first as an editorial assistant at New Market Press before becoming one of the editors at Harper Collins Publishers. He knows how to write and what will become a bestseller. Within Harper Collins Publishers, Papasan worked on bestsellers such as *Go for the Goal* by Mia Hamm and *Body-for-Life* by Bill Phillips. Not only did he work with successful authors, but Papasan also co-owned his own successful real estate team that had affiliation with Keller Williams Realty with his wife. With his knowledge for books and real estate, Jay Papasan helped co-author the *Millionaire Real Estate* series along with Gary Keller as well as *The ONE Thing*.

Papasan is also the Vice President of publishing and the executive editor at KellerINK, the publishing side of the Keller Williams Realty. In the year 2014, Jay Papasan was named one of the *Most Powerful People in Real Estate* by Swanepoel Power 200, the official annual ranking of residential real estate in North America.

Fireside Questions

"What would you do?"

Tip: These questions can be a fun exercise as it spurs creativity among the readers by allowing alternate scene endings and "if this was you" questions.

question 21

Gary Keller first worked at another real estate company and made it his goal to become VP. How important do you feel it is to set goals such as that and to work towards them?

question 22

Once Keller became VP at his first real estate company, he realized he couldn't work there and chose to create his own company that supported their agents better. How do you feel as an employee that Keller did this?

~~~

question 23

Keller co-authored his real estate books so that others could learn their techniques and become better agents themselves, even if they didn't work for his company. How do you think other agents felt when they learned this? What about other company owners?

~~~

question 24

Jay Papasan worked with books as an editor in two different publishing houses. How do you feel this helped him co-author with Keller?

~~~

question 25

Jay Papasan was nominated as one of the most powerful people in real estate. How do you think he felt when he received that nomination?

~~~

~~~

question 26

One of the book's lessons is that in order to move forward, one should listen to those who are at the end of their life and the regrets they may have. If you had received news of your future death, what would you regret?

~~~

~ ~ ~

question 27

Jay Papasan received his opportunity to co-author with Keller due to having edited Keller's previous books at Harper Collins Publishing. How do you think you would feel if you knew your boss was writing another book after you had previously edited his others?

~ ~ ~

~~~

question 28

Gary Keller became known for his real estate businesses. Do you think he would have had as much success if he had a career in something else? Why or why not?

~~~

question 29

Jay Papasan worked as an editor at Harper Collins Publishing. What do you think would have happened if he had stayed at Harper Collins?

~~~

question 30

Gary Keller wrote three books to help real estate agents be even better at their jobs. How do you think those books would have been received if he had been published in England instead of America?

~~~

Quiz Questions

"Ready to Announce the Winners?"

Tip: Create a leaderboard and track scores to see who gets the most correct answers. Winners required. Prizes optional.

quiz question 1

True/False: The book *The ONE Thing* is sectioned into three sections.

quiz question 2

True/False: It is urged for a person to work on their One Thing for only two hours every day.

~~~

quiz question 3

Inspiration was taken from Vilfredo Pareto, a famous _____.

~~~

quiz question 4

True/False: Vilfredo Pareto's philosophy is about how to apply work effort for results.

quiz question 5

True/False: Vilfredo Pareto's philosophy states that with 10% work produces 90% results.

quiz question 6

True/False: the One Thing that a person does can be multiple steps to reach a goal.

~~~

quiz question 7

Keller and Papasan stated that achieving a perfect balance between work/home life is _____.

quiz question 8

True/False: Before creating Keller Williams Realty, Keller had only worked as a real estate agent.

~ ~ ~

~~~

quiz question 9

True/False: One of the suggestions from *The ONE Thing* is to listen to the regrets of those who are at the end of their lives.

~~~

quiz question 10

Jay Papasan had previously worked at _____ before Harper Collins Publishers.

~~~

quiz question 11

True/False: Jay Papasan edited Gary Kellers previous books while working at New Market Press.

~~~

quiz question 12

Jay Papasan was named one of the *Most Powerful People in Real Estate* in the year _____.

Quiz Answers

1. True
2. False
3. Economist
4. True
5. False
6. True
7. Unrealistic
8. False
9. True
10. New Market Press
11. False
12. 2014

Ways to Continue Your Reading

EVERY month, our team runs through a wide selection of books to pick the best titles for readers and reading groups, and promotes these titles to our thousands of readers – sometimes with free downloads, sale dates, and additional brochures.

If you have not yet read the original work or would like to read it again, <u>get the book here.</u>

Want to register yourself or a book group? It's free and takes 1-click.

Register here.

On the Next Page...

Please write us your reviews! Any length would be fine but we'd appreciate hearing you more! We'd be SO grateful.

Till next time,

BookHabits

"Loving Books is Actually a Habit"